THIS JOURNAL BELONGS TO

THE FORAGER'S JOURNAL

HOW TO USE THIS BOOK

WELCOME TO YOUR FORAGING JOURNAL, a place to record everything about your wild food adventures.

This field notebook is divided into three parts. First are the Foraging Logs, which are the heart of the journal. Here, you have a place to record details about specific outings. Each log entry includes prompts for key information, such as the date, location, time of day, environment, and weather. Use the notes section to record whom you were with or unique aspects of the day. A grid is provided to record the wild plants you've identified and collected, as well as the ones you haven't. By recording the description and location of plants and fungi you don't recognize, you can use that information to look them up later. Each log also includes a blank page for sketches and a place to document photography or video you may have taken during your outing. Designate a Log # for each session to correlate with your entries in the Foraging Log Index found on the next few pages. This way, every excursion will be easy to find and reference.

Following the logs, there's a section with blank pages where you can include additional notes or drawings—map your favorite foraging locale, sketch your prized finds, or just reminisce about a particularly memorable experience.

The final section, Foraging Lists, gives you a place to keep tabs on the edible plants found in your own backyard, a wish list of wild foods you hope to gather someday, and a bucket list of foraging destinations.

HAPPY FORAGING!

FORAGING LOGS

FORAGING LOG INDEX

LOG #	LOCATION	DATE

LOG #	LOCATION	DATE

FORAGING LOG INDEX

LOG #	LOCATION	DATE

LOG #	LOCATION	DATE

FORAGING LOG

LOG #

DATE

LOCATION

START TIME

END TIME

HABITAT

WEATHER

NOTES ON THE DAY

SKETCHES

EDIBLE PLANTS AND FUNGI I IDENTIFIED

NAME/DESCRIPTION	HOW MANY I COLLECTED

PICTURES/VIDEOS I TOOK (file name) ______________________

____

____

____

OVERALL RATING OF THE DAY

FORAGING LOG

LOG #

DATE

LOCATION

START TIME

END TIME

HABITAT

WEATHER

NOTES ON THE DAY

SKETCHES

EDIBLE PLANTS AND FUNGI I IDENTIFIED

NAME/DESCRIPTION	HOW MANY I COLLECTED

PICTURES/VIDEOS I TOOK (file name)

OVERALL RATING OF THE DAY

FORAGING LOG

LOG #

DATE

LOCATION

START TIME

END TIME

HABITAT

WEATHER

NOTES ON THE DAY

SKETCHES

EDIBLE PLANTS AND FUNGI I IDENTIFIED

NAME/DESCRIPTION	HOW MANY I COLLECTED

PICTURES/VIDEOS I TOOK (file name) ______________________

____

____

____

OVERALL RATING OF THE DAY

FORAGING LOG

LOG #

DATE

LOCATION

START TIME

END TIME

HABITAT

WEATHER

NOTES ON THE DAY

SKETCHES

EDIBLE PLANTS AND FUNGI I IDENTIFIED

NAME/DESCRIPTION	HOW MANY I COLLECTED

PICTURES/VIDEOS I TOOK (file name) ______________________________

____

____

____

OVERALL RATING OF THE DAY

FORAGING LOG

LOG #

DATE

LOCATION

START TIME

END TIME

HABITAT

WEATHER

NOTES ON THE DAY

SKETCHES

EDIBLE PLANTS AND FUNGI I IDENTIFIED

NAME/DESCRIPTION	HOW MANY I COLLECTED

PICTURES/VIDEOS I TOOK (file name) ____________________

____

____

____

OVERALL RATING OF THE DAY

FORAGING LOG

LOG #

DATE

LOCATION

START TIME

END TIME

HABITAT

WEATHER

NOTES ON THE DAY

SKETCHES

EDIBLE PLANTS AND FUNGI I IDENTIFIED

NAME/DESCRIPTION	HOW MANY I COLLECTED

PICTURES/VIDEOS I TOOK (file name) ______________________

____

____

____

OVERALL RATING OF THE DAY

FORAGING LOG

LOG #

DATE

LOCATION

START TIME

END TIME

HABITAT

WEATHER

NOTES ON THE DAY

SKETCHES

EDIBLE PLANTS AND FUNGI I IDENTIFIED

NAME/DESCRIPTION	HOW MANY I COLLECTED

PICTURES/VIDEOS I TOOK (file name) ______________________________

____

____

____

OVERALL RATING OF THE DAY

FORAGING LOG

LOG #

DATE

LOCATION

START TIME

END TIME

HABITAT

WEATHER

NOTES ON THE DAY

SKETCHES

EDIBLE PLANTS AND FUNGI I IDENTIFIED

NAME/DESCRIPTION	HOW MANY I COLLECTED

PICTURES/VIDEOS I TOOK (file name) ______________________________

____

____

____

OVERALL RATING OF THE DAY

FORAGING LOG

LOG #

DATE

LOCATION

START TIME

END TIME

HABITAT

WEATHER

NOTES ON THE DAY

SKETCHES

EDIBLE PLANTS AND FUNGI I IDENTIFIED

NAME/DESCRIPTION	HOW MANY I COLLECTED

PICTURES/VIDEOS I TOOK (file name) ______________________

____

____

____

OVERALL RATING OF THE DAY

FORAGING LOG

LOG #

DATE

LOCATION

START TIME

END TIME

HABITAT

WEATHER

NOTES ON THE DAY

SKETCHES

EDIBLE PLANTS AND FUNGI I IDENTIFIED

NAME/DESCRIPTION	HOW MANY I COLLECTED

PICTURES/VIDEOS I TOOK (file name) ______________________

____

____

____

OVERALL RATING OF THE DAY

FORAGING LOG

LOG #

DATE

LOCATION

START TIME

END TIME

HABITAT

WEATHER

NOTES ON THE DAY

SKETCHES

EDIBLE PLANTS AND FUNGI I IDENTIFIED

NAME/DESCRIPTION	HOW MANY I COLLECTED

PICTURES/VIDEOS I TOOK (file name)

OVERALL RATING OF THE DAY

FORAGING LOG

LOG #

DATE

LOCATION

START TIME

END TIME

HABITAT

WEATHER

NOTES ON THE DAY

SKETCHES

EDIBLE PLANTS AND FUNGI I IDENTIFIED

NAME/DESCRIPTION	HOW MANY I COLLECTED

PICTURES/VIDEOS I TOOK (file name) ______________________

____

____

____

OVERALL RATING OF THE DAY

FORAGING LOG

LOG #

DATE

LOCATION

START TIME

END TIME

HABITAT

WEATHER

NOTES ON THE DAY

SKETCHES

EDIBLE PLANTS AND FUNGI I IDENTIFIED

NAME/DESCRIPTION	HOW MANY I COLLECTED

PICTURES/VIDEOS I TOOK (file name) ______________________________

____

____

____

OVERALL RATING OF THE DAY

FORAGING LOG

LOG #

DATE

LOCATION

START TIME

END TIME

HABITAT

WEATHER

NOTES ON THE DAY

SKETCHES

EDIBLE PLANTS AND FUNGI I IDENTIFIED

NAME/DESCRIPTION	HOW MANY I COLLECTED

PICTURES/VIDEOS I TOOK (file name) ______________________

____

____

____

OVERALL RATING OF THE DAY

FORAGING LOG

LOG #

DATE

LOCATION

START TIME

END TIME

HABITAT

WEATHER

NOTES ON THE DAY

SKETCHES

EDIBLE PLANTS AND FUNGI I IDENTIFIED

NAME/DESCRIPTION	HOW MANY I COLLECTED

PICTURES/VIDEOS I TOOK (file name) ______________________

____

____

____

OVERALL RATING OF THE DAY

FORAGING LOG

LOG #

DATE

LOCATION

START TIME

END TIME

HABITAT

WEATHER

NOTES ON THE DAY

SKETCHES

EDIBLE PLANTS AND FUNGI I IDENTIFIED

NAME/DESCRIPTION	HOW MANY I COLLECTED

PICTURES/VIDEOS I TOOK (file name) ______________________________

____

____

____

OVERALL RATING OF THE DAY

FORAGING LOG

LOG #

DATE

LOCATION

START TIME

END TIME

HABITAT

WEATHER

NOTES ON THE DAY

SKETCHES

EDIBLE PLANTS AND FUNGI I IDENTIFIED

NAME/DESCRIPTION	HOW MANY I COLLECTED

PICTURES/VIDEOS I TOOK (file name) ______________________________

____

____

____

OVERALL RATING OF THE DAY

FORAGING LOG

LOG #

DATE

LOCATION

START TIME

END TIME

HABITAT

WEATHER

NOTES ON THE DAY

SKETCHES

EDIBLE PLANTS AND FUNGI I IDENTIFIED

NAME/DESCRIPTION	HOW MANY I COLLECTED

PICTURES/VIDEOS I TOOK (file name) ______________________

____

____

____

OVERALL RATING OF THE DAY

FORAGING LOG

LOG #

DATE

LOCATION

START TIME

END TIME

HABITAT

WEATHER

NOTES ON THE DAY

SKETCHES

EDIBLE PLANTS AND FUNGI I IDENTIFIED

NAME/DESCRIPTION	HOW MANY I COLLECTED

PICTURES/VIDEOS I TOOK (file name) ______________________

____

____

____

OVERALL RATING OF THE DAY

FORAGING LOG

LOG #

DATE

LOCATION

START TIME

END TIME

HABITAT

WEATHER

NOTES ON THE DAY

SKETCHES

EDIBLE PLANTS AND FUNGI I IDENTIFIED

NAME/DESCRIPTION	HOW MANY I COLLECTED

PICTURES/VIDEOS I TOOK (file name) ______________________

____

____

____

OVERALL RATING OF THE DAY

FORAGING LOG

LOG #

DATE

LOCATION

START TIME

END TIME

HABITAT

WEATHER

NOTES ON THE DAY

SKETCHES

EDIBLE PLANTS AND FUNGI I IDENTIFIED

NAME/DESCRIPTION	HOW MANY I COLLECTED

PICTURES/VIDEOS I TOOK (file name) ______________________________

____

____

____

OVERALL RATING OF THE DAY

FORAGING LOG

LOG #

DATE

LOCATION

START TIME

END TIME

HABITAT

WEATHER

NOTES ON THE DAY

SKETCHES

EDIBLE PLANTS AND FUNGI I IDENTIFIED

NAME/DESCRIPTION	HOW MANY I COLLECTED

PICTURES/VIDEOS I TOOK (file name) ____________________

____

____

____

OVERALL RATING OF THE DAY

FORAGING LOG

LOG #

DATE

LOCATION

START TIME

END TIME

HABITAT

WEATHER

NOTES ON THE DAY

SKETCHES

EDIBLE PLANTS AND FUNGI I IDENTIFIED

NAME/DESCRIPTION	HOW MANY I COLLECTED

PICTURES/VIDEOS I TOOK (file name) ______________________

____

____

____

OVERALL RATING OF THE DAY

FORAGING LOG

LOG #

DATE

LOCATION

START TIME

END TIME

HABITAT

WEATHER

NOTES ON THE DAY

SKETCHES

EDIBLE PLANTS AND FUNGI I IDENTIFIED

NAME/DESCRIPTION	HOW MANY I COLLECTED

PICTURES/VIDEOS I TOOK (file name) ______________________

____

____

____

OVERALL RATING OF THE DAY

FORAGING LOG

LOG #

DATE

LOCATION

START TIME

END TIME

HABITAT

WEATHER

NOTES ON THE DAY

SKETCHES

EDIBLE PLANTS AND FUNGI I IDENTIFIED

NAME/DESCRIPTION	HOW MANY I COLLECTED

PICTURES/VIDEOS I TOOK (file name) ____________________

____

____

____

OVERALL RATING OF THE DAY

FORAGING LOG

LOG #

DATE

LOCATION

START TIME

END TIME

HABITAT

WEATHER

NOTES ON THE DAY

SKETCHES

EDIBLE PLANTS AND FUNGI I IDENTIFIED

NAME/DESCRIPTION	HOW MANY I COLLECTED

PICTURES/VIDEOS I TOOK (file name) ______________________________

____

____

____

OVERALL RATING OF THE DAY

FORAGING LOG

LOG #

DATE

LOCATION

START TIME

END TIME

HABITAT

WEATHER

NOTES ON THE DAY

SKETCHES

EDIBLE PLANTS AND FUNGI I IDENTIFIED

NAME/DESCRIPTION	HOW MANY I COLLECTED

PICTURES/VIDEOS I TOOK (file name) ______________________

____

____

____

OVERALL RATING OF THE DAY

FORAGING LOG

LOG #

DATE

LOCATION

START TIME

END TIME

HABITAT

WEATHER

NOTES ON THE DAY

SKETCHES

EDIBLE PLANTS AND FUNGI I IDENTIFIED

NAME/DESCRIPTION	HOW MANY I COLLECTED

PICTURES/VIDEOS I TOOK (file name) ____________________

____

____

____

OVERALL RATING OF THE DAY

FORAGING LOG

LOG #

DATE

LOCATION

START TIME

END TIME

HABITAT

WEATHER

NOTES ON THE DAY

SKETCHES

EDIBLE PLANTS AND FUNGI I IDENTIFIED

NAME/DESCRIPTION	HOW MANY I COLLECTED

PICTURES/VIDEOS I TOOK (file name) ______________________

____

____

____

OVERALL RATING OF THE DAY

FORAGING LOG

LOG #

DATE

LOCATION

START TIME

END TIME

HABITAT

WEATHER

NOTES ON THE DAY

SKETCHES

EDIBLE PLANTS AND FUNGI I IDENTIFIED

NAME/DESCRIPTION	HOW MANY I COLLECTED

PICTURES/VIDEOS I TOOK (file name) ______________________

____

____

____

OVERALL RATING OF THE DAY

FORAGING LOG

LOG #

DATE

LOCATION

START TIME

END TIME

HABITAT

WEATHER

NOTES ON THE DAY

SKETCHES

EDIBLE PLANTS AND FUNGI I IDENTIFIED

NAME/DESCRIPTION	HOW MANY I COLLECTED

PICTURES/VIDEOS I TOOK (file name) ______________________

____

____

____

OVERALL RATING OF THE DAY

FORAGING LOG

LOG #

DATE

LOCATION

START TIME

END TIME

HABITAT

WEATHER

NOTES ON THE DAY

SKETCHES

EDIBLE PLANTS AND FUNGI I IDENTIFIED

NAME/DESCRIPTION	HOW MANY I COLLECTED

PICTURES/VIDEOS I TOOK (file name) ____________________

____

____

____

OVERALL RATING OF THE DAY

FORAGING LOG

LOG #

DATE

LOCATION

START TIME

END TIME

HABITAT

WEATHER

NOTES ON THE DAY

SKETCHES

EDIBLE PLANTS AND FUNGI I IDENTIFIED

NAME/DESCRIPTION	HOW MANY I COLLECTED

PICTURES/VIDEOS I TOOK (file name) ______________________________

____

____

____

OVERALL RATING OF THE DAY

FORAGING LOG

LOG #

DATE

LOCATION

START TIME

END TIME

HABITAT

WEATHER

NOTES ON THE DAY

SKETCHES

EDIBLE PLANTS AND FUNGI I IDENTIFIED

NAME/DESCRIPTION	HOW MANY I COLLECTED

PICTURES/VIDEOS I TOOK (file name) ______________________

____

____

____

OVERALL RATING OF THE DAY

FORAGING LOG

LOG #

DATE

LOCATION

START TIME

END TIME

HABITAT

WEATHER

NOTES ON THE DAY

SKETCHES

EDIBLE PLANTS AND FUNGI I IDENTIFIED

NAME/DESCRIPTION	HOW MANY I COLLECTED

PICTURES/VIDEOS I TOOK (file name) ______________________________

____

____

____

OVERALL RATING OF THE DAY

FORAGING LOG

LOG #

DATE

LOCATION

START TIME

END TIME

HABITAT

WEATHER

NOTES ON THE DAY

SKETCHES

EDIBLE PLANTS AND FUNGI I IDENTIFIED

NAME/DESCRIPTION	HOW MANY I COLLECTED

PICTURES/VIDEOS I TOOK (file name) ______________________

____

____

____

OVERALL RATING OF THE DAY

FORAGING LOG

LOG #

DATE

LOCATION

START TIME

END TIME

HABITAT

WEATHER

NOTES ON THE DAY

SKETCHES

EDIBLE PLANTS AND FUNGI I IDENTIFIED

NAME/DESCRIPTION	HOW MANY I COLLECTED

PICTURES/VIDEOS I TOOK (file name) ______________________________

____

____

____

OVERALL RATING OF THE DAY

FORAGING LOG

LOG #

DATE

LOCATION

START TIME

END TIME

HABITAT

WEATHER

NOTES ON THE DAY

SKETCHES

EDIBLE PLANTS AND FUNGI I IDENTIFIED

NAME/DESCRIPTION	HOW MANY I COLLECTED

PICTURES/VIDEOS I TOOK (file name) ______________________________

____

____

____

OVERALL RATING OF THE DAY

FORAGING LOG

LOG #

DATE

LOCATION

START TIME

END TIME

HABITAT

WEATHER

NOTES ON THE DAY

SKETCHES

EDIBLE PLANTS AND FUNGI I IDENTIFIED

NAME/DESCRIPTION	HOW MANY I COLLECTED

PICTURES/VIDEOS I TOOK (file name) ______________________________

____

____

____

OVERALL RATING OF THE DAY

FORAGING LOG

LOG #

DATE

LOCATION

START TIME

END TIME

HABITAT

WEATHER

NOTES ON THE DAY

SKETCHES

EDIBLE PLANTS AND FUNGI I IDENTIFIED

NAME/DESCRIPTION	HOW MANY I COLLECTED

PICTURES/VIDEOS I TOOK (file name) ______________________

____

____

____

OVERALL RATING OF THE DAY

FORAGING LOG

LOG #

DATE

LOCATION

START TIME

END TIME

HABITAT

WEATHER

NOTES ON THE DAY

SKETCHES

EDIBLE PLANTS AND FUNGI I IDENTIFIED

NAME/DESCRIPTION	HOW MANY I COLLECTED

PICTURES/VIDEOS I TOOK (file name) ____________________

OVERALL RATING OF THE DAY

FORAGING LOG

LOG #

DATE

LOCATION

START TIME

END TIME

HABITAT

WEATHER

NOTES ON THE DAY

SKETCHES

EDIBLE PLANTS AND FUNGI I IDENTIFIED

NAME/DESCRIPTION	HOW MANY I COLLECTED

PICTURES/VIDEOS I TOOK (file name) ______________________________

____

____

____

OVERALL RATING OF THE DAY

FORAGING LOG

LOG #

DATE

LOCATION

START TIME

END TIME

HABITAT

WEATHER

NOTES ON THE DAY

SKETCHES

EDIBLE PLANTS AND FUNGI I IDENTIFIED

NAME/DESCRIPTION	HOW MANY I COLLECTED

PICTURES/VIDEOS I TOOK (file name) ____________________

____

____

____

OVERALL RATING OF THE DAY

FORAGING LOG

LOG #

DATE

LOCATION

START TIME

END TIME

HABITAT

WEATHER

NOTES ON THE DAY

SKETCHES

EDIBLE PLANTS AND FUNGI I IDENTIFIED

NAME/DESCRIPTION	HOW MANY I COLLECTED

PICTURES/VIDEOS I TOOK (file name) ______________________________

____

____

____

OVERALL RATING OF THE DAY

FORAGING LOG

LOG #

DATE

LOCATION

START TIME

END TIME

HABITAT

WEATHER

NOTES ON THE DAY

SKETCHES

EDIBLE PLANTS AND FUNGI I IDENTIFIED

NAME/DESCRIPTION	HOW MANY I COLLECTED

PICTURES/VIDEOS I TOOK (file name) ______________________

____

____

____

OVERALL RATING OF THE DAY

FORAGING LOG

LOG #

DATE

LOCATION

START TIME

END TIME

HABITAT

WEATHER

NOTES ON THE DAY

SKETCHES

EDIBLE PLANTS AND FUNGI I IDENTIFIED

NAME/DESCRIPTION	HOW MANY I COLLECTED

PICTURES/VIDEOS I TOOK (file name) ____________________

____

____

____

OVERALL RATING OF THE DAY

FORAGING LOG

LOG #

DATE

LOCATION

START TIME

END TIME

HABITAT

WEATHER

NOTES ON THE DAY

SKETCHES

EDIBLE PLANTS AND FUNGI I IDENTIFIED

NAME/DESCRIPTION	HOW MANY I COLLECTED

PICTURES/VIDEOS I TOOK (file name) ____________________

____

____

____

OVERALL RATING OF THE DAY

FORAGING LOG

LOG #

DATE

LOCATION

START TIME

END TIME

HABITAT

WEATHER

NOTES ON THE DAY

SKETCHES

EDIBLE PLANTS AND FUNGI I IDENTIFIED

NAME/DESCRIPTION	HOW MANY I COLLECTED

PICTURES/VIDEOS I TOOK (file name) ______________________

____

____

____

OVERALL RATING OF THE DAY

FORAGING LOG

LOG #

DATE

LOCATION

START TIME

END TIME

HABITAT

WEATHER

NOTES ON THE DAY

SKETCHES

EDIBLE PLANTS AND FUNGI I IDENTIFIED

NAME/DESCRIPTION	HOW MANY I COLLECTED

PICTURES/VIDEOS I TOOK (file name) ____________________

____

____

____

OVERALL RATING OF THE DAY

FORAGING LOG

LOG #

DATE

LOCATION

START TIME

END TIME

HABITAT

WEATHER

NOTES ON THE DAY

SKETCHES

EDIBLE PLANTS AND FUNGI I IDENTIFIED

NAME/DESCRIPTION	HOW MANY I COLLECTED

PICTURES/VIDEOS I TOOK (file name) ______________________________

____

____

____

OVERALL RATING OF THE DAY

FORAGING LOG

LOG #

DATE

LOCATION

START TIME

END TIME

HABITAT

WEATHER

NOTES ON THE DAY

SKETCHES

EDIBLE PLANTS AND FUNGI I IDENTIFIED

NAME/DESCRIPTION	HOW MANY I COLLECTED

PICTURES/VIDEOS I TOOK (file name) ______

OVERALL RATING OF THE DAY

FORAGING LOG

LOG #

DATE

LOCATION

START TIME

END TIME

HABITAT

WEATHER

NOTES ON THE DAY

SKETCHES

EDIBLE PLANTS AND FUNGI I IDENTIFIED

NAME/DESCRIPTION	HOW MANY I COLLECTED

PICTURES/VIDEOS I TOOK (file name) ______________________

____

____

____

OVERALL RATING OF THE DAY

FORAGING LOG

LOG #

DATE

LOCATION

START TIME

END TIME

HABITAT

WEATHER

NOTES ON THE DAY

SKETCHES

EDIBLE PLANTS AND FUNGI I IDENTIFIED

NAME/DESCRIPTION	HOW MANY I COLLECTED

PICTURES/VIDEOS I TOOK (file name) ____________________

OVERALL RATING OF THE DAY

FORAGING LOG

LOG #

DATE

LOCATION

START TIME

END TIME

HABITAT

WEATHER

NOTES ON THE DAY

SKETCHES

EDIBLE PLANTS AND FUNGI I IDENTIFIED

NAME/DESCRIPTION	HOW MANY I COLLECTED

PICTURES/VIDEOS I TOOK (file name) ______________________________

____

____

____

OVERALL RATING OF THE DAY

FORAGING LOG

LOG #

DATE

LOCATION

START TIME

END TIME

HABITAT

WEATHER

NOTES ON THE DAY

SKETCHES

EDIBLE PLANTS AND FUNGI I IDENTIFIED

NAME/DESCRIPTION	HOW MANY I COLLECTED

PICTURES/VIDEOS I TOOK (file name) ______________________________

____

____

____

OVERALL RATING OF THE DAY

NOTES & SKETCHES

"UNTIL WE CAN COMPREHEND THE BEGUILING BEAUTY OF A SINGLE FLOWER, WE ARE WOEFULLY UNABLE TO GRASP THE MEANING AND POTENTIAL OF LIFE ITSELF."

—Virginia Woolf

"READING ABOUT NATURE IS FINE, BUT IF A PERSON WALKS IN THE WOODS AND LISTENS CAREFULLY, HE CAN LEARN MORE THAN WHAT IS IN BOOKS, FOR THEY SPEAK WITH THE VOICE OF GOD."

—George Washington Carver

"NATURE ALONE IS ANTIQUE, AND THE OLDEST ART A MUSHROOM."

—Thomas Carlyle

"BEAUTIFUL AS A DANDELION-BLOSSOM, GOLDEN IN THE GREEN GRASS, THIS LIFE CAN BE."

—Edna St. Vincent Millay

"IN ALL THINGS OF NATURE THERE IS SOMETHING OF THE MARVELOUS."

—Aristotle

"I'VE ALWAYS THOUGHT FAIRIES ARE LIKE MUSHROOMS. YOU TRIP OVER THEM WHEN YOU'RE NOT THINKING ABOUT THEM, BUT THEY'RE HARD TO SPOT WHEN YOU'RE SEARCHING FOR THEM."

—Jo Walton

"WHAT IS A WEED? A PLANT WHOSE VIRTUES HAVE NEVER BEEN DISCOVERED."

—Ralph Waldo Emerson

"I HAVE LOST MY SMILE, BUT DON'T WORRY. THE DANDELION HAS IT."

—Thich Nhat Hanh

"ATTEND TO MUSHROOMS AND ALL OTHER THINGS WILL ANSWER UP."

—A. R. Ammons

“LOOK DEEP INTO NATURE, AND THEN YOU WILL UNDERSTAND EVERYTHING BETTER.”

—Albert Einstein

FORAGING LISTS

BACKYARD FORAGING

SOMETIMES THE MOST MEMORABLE FORAGING EXPERIENCES occur right outside our door. Compile a list here of the plants and fungi you have enjoyed gathering close to home.

PLANT/FUNGUS	DATE/TIME	NOTES

MY FORAGING WISH LIST

RECORD THE EDIBLE PLANTS AND FUNGI you hope to forage in your lifetime here, and check them off when you are lucky enough to find them.

- [ ]
- [ ]
- [ ]
- [ ]
- [ ]
- [ ]
- [ ]
- [ ]
- [ ]
- [ ]
- [ ]
- [ ]
- [ ]
- [ ]
- [ ]
- [ ]
- [ ]
- [ ]
- [ ]
- [ ]
- [ ]

MY FORAGING DESTINATIONS

FROM CONSERVATION LAND TO MANY STATE AND NATIONAL PARKS, there are so many worthy places across the globe ripe for foraging. Are there places you hope to travel to in order to see a particular plant or fungus? Record the details here.

DESTINATION **SEASON**

EDIBLE PLANTS/FUNGI I HOPE TO FIND

NOTES

☐ TRIP PLANNED

DESTINATION **SEASON**

EDIBLE PLANTS/FUNGI I HOPE TO FIND

NOTES

☐ TRIP PLANNED

DESTINATION | SEASON

EDIBLE PLANTS/FUNGI I HOPE TO FIND

NOTES

☐ TRIP PLANNED

DESTINATION | SEASON

EDIBLE PLANTS/FUNGI I HOPE TO FIND

NOTES

☐ TRIP PLANNED

DESTINATION | SEASON

EDIBLE PLANTS/FUNGI I HOPE TO FIND

NOTES

☐ TRIP PLANNED

THE FORAGER'S JOURNAL

weldonowen

www.weldonowen.com

The information provided in this book is strictly for reference only and is not in any manner a substitute for proper nutritional or medical advice. Always follow local foraging regulations.

ISBN: 979-8-88674-170-4

PRINTED IN CHINA

10 9 8 7 6 5 4 3 2 1